BENJI'S BEEING BOOK

IMAGINED BY DR. BOBBY BUKA
ILLUSTRATED BY ALEJANDRO GIRALDO

"To the first Benji, and his very next adventure.
To Jesse, whose thoughtfulness and love light us up everyday.
And to Grandma Joy, who taught us both how to parent with
patience and wonder." - B.B.

Copyright © 2020 by Bobby Buka

ISBN: 978-0-578-77511-1

Library of Congress Control Number is on file with Library of Congress.

All Rights Reserved. No part of this book may be reproduced or transmitted in any form or by any means, electronic or mechanical, including photocopying, recording, or by any information storage and retrieval system without written permission from the author, except for the inclusion of brief quotations in a review.

Printed in the United States of America.

All over the world,

in nooks and crannies near

blooming flowers everywhere,

are hives just like this one,

full of busy bees.

Benji is a bee.

He lives here too.

Inside the hive,
bees would buzz here and
bees would buzz there.

Collecting nectar,
making honey,
building wax,
nobody ever seemed
to stand still.

Nobody, that is,
except for Benji.

Benji worked at his own pace. He spent time learning about all sorts of different blossoms. Hibiscus! Geranium! Marigold!

After studying flowers, Benji would fall asleep on top of their petals, dreaming of a place far away from the hustle-bustle of the hive.

Back at the tree, bees kept their noses to the grindstone. Work, work, work! And while Benji snoozed in a nearby lily, the Queen Bee surprised everyone with a big announcement:

"Our home is too crowded. Everybody gather your files, collect your notes, and pack your bags! Tonight we find a new spot for a bigger, better hive!"

And swarm they did...

into the night sky!

Benji awoke the next morning, and flew his way back to find an empty hive. 'This place is usually packed,' he thought, 'but today it is really quiet and somebody left the snack room a mess!'
This was a strange day indeed.

Benji needed to think.

He took a sip of nectar juice.

He waited so long that he drank through a whole case...but still no one showed up.

With everyone gone, who would report on all the flower visits, who would send news on the beeswax built, and who would give updates to the Queen!?

"I'll get to work," said Benji aloud. "The flowers need visiting, the nectar needs collecting, and The Queen needs her news!" Benji checked his b-mail. There was a message from Anton.

"Hey Bee Bro."

Benji spun around to find Anton in his hiveway. Whoa, that was fast.

"Look at all this empty space!" said Anton.

"I know," said Benji Bee, "grab a stump and have a seat! We can play video games and drink nectar juice."

And just like that, Anton moved in.

And two old friends played darts together.

They listened to records, and played soccer all day, every day, until the moon rose.

Days passed
and then weeks.
Anton invited a bunch
of his friends over
and things started to get
pretty busy again.

In fact, ants soon filled
the entire hive.
They could not make
honey nor wax, but
they were really good
at filling the place
with extra stuff.

Benji figured the hive was busier now, and louder, than it had ever been before.

The construction noises of busy ants had replaced the buzz of his fellow bees.

'Oh dear,' Benji thought, 'time to head back to my flower patch for some peace and quiet.'

Benji found a quiet spot down the road by the river.

It was peaceful here, and he had everything he could wish for.

"What kind of flower is that?" asked Ladybug Janice.

"Oh that's a lily," said Benji, "pass the popcorn please."

Back at the hive, Anton and his fellow ants were running out of space!

Things had gotten so popular here that ants had come from miles away only to find there wasn't much room left.

Now the hive was way too crowded and not very fun to live in.

One day, Benji saw Anton coming down the road. He looked tired.

"What happened, Anton, why have you left the hive?" Benji asked.

Anton said, "Benji Buddy, this busy life is not for me either. I like your style!"

And with that, two good friends headed up the hill for some fresh air and bright stars.

The gang gathered

on top of the grassy hill.

They counted stars and

wished on the falling ones.

All sat for a moment

of stillness in the grass

...and took a nice long

sip of nectar juice.

THE END